Paycheck to Prosperity:

A Comprehensive Guide to Managing Your Money and Maximizing Your Wealth

By

Ann R. Disanto

TABLE OF CONTENTS

INTRODUCTION

Welcome to "Paycheck to Prosperity: A Comprehensive __Guide to Managing Your Money and Maximizing Your Wealth." If you're reading this, chances are you're looking to gain control of your financial future, elevate your monetary__ situation, and maximize your earning potential. You're in the right place. This book is designed to empower you with knowledge, equip_ you with actionable__ strategies, and inspire you to take the helm of your financial journey.

Our journey into financial__ independence is, more often than not, a journey of self-discovery and self-empowerment. With every dollar we earn, spend, save, invest, or donate, we make decisions that can either__ inch us closer to our goals or set us further back. Yet, many of us tread on this path with little to no understanding of how to manage our finances effectively. The lack of financial__ education has left many feeling lost, overwhelmed, or trapped in a never-ending cycle of paycheck-to-paycheck living.

That's where this_ book comes in.

"Paycheck to Prosperity" isn't just about managing your money; it's about transforming your __relationship with money. It's about understanding that each paycheck you earn isn't merely a means to an end, but a tool to build the life you envision for yourself. It's about breaking free from the__ paycheck-to-paycheck cycle and opening doors to wealth accumulation and financial peace of mind.

Throughout this guide, we will delve into various__ facets of personal finance - from understanding your income and budgeting to saving, investing, and planning for retirement. We will also tackle complex issues like debt__ management, tax planning, and estate planning in a straightforward, easy-to-understand manner. Moreover, we will explore the psychological__ aspects of financial decisions and provide insights into making rational, beneficial choices.

Remember, the journey to financial independence isn't a race; it's a personal journey that moves at a pace unique to each__ individual. It doesn't matter where you're starting from; what matters is your commitment to embark on this journey and your perseverance to stay the course.

So, let's turn the page and take that first step towards __transforming your paycheck into prosperity. I'M

THRILLED TO BE YOUR GUIDE ON THIS EXCITING JOURNEY. *Let's get started!*

Chapter 1: The Power of Financial Planning: Delve into the Importance of Planning, Setting Financial ___Goals, and Understanding Your Current Financial Standing

Financial planning is the cornerstone of achieving financial__ health, stability, and growth. Let's delve into the significance of planning, setting_ goals, and understanding your current financial position:

- **The Importance of Financial Planning:** Financial planning allows you to make informed decisions about your money, aligning your financial __actions with your life goals. It provides a roadmap for your financial _journey, helping you to manage income, savings, and expenditures effectively.

- **Setting Financial Goals:** Your financial goals are a key aspect of your financial plan. These__ goals, which can be short, medium, or long term, give you a clear direction and purpose for your financial decisions. Examples include saving for a vacation, buying a home, or preparing for retirement.

- **Understanding Your Current Financial Standing:** To _create a financial plan, you need a clear picture of your current financial situation. This involves assessing all_ aspects of your finances, including income, expenses, assets, debts, and net worth. By understanding your financial standing, you can identify _areas of strength and areas that need improvement.

- **Creating a Financial Plan:** Creating a financial plan involves establishing your financial __goals, assessing your current financial situation, creating a budget, planning for savings and investments, managing debts, and planning for tax and retirement. Your financial__ plan is a dynamic document that should evolve with changes in your life and financial situation.

- **The Power of Financial Planning:** The power of financial__ planning lies in its ability to provide you with financial confidence and control. A good financial plan will guide you towards financial stability and __growth, allowing you to navigate financial challenges, take advantage of opportunities, and achieve your life goals.

Remember, while financial planning can seem complex, breaking it down into manageable__ steps can make the process much more approachable. Consider seeking professional__ advice if needed, but remember that no one knows your financial goals and priorities better than you.

Chapter 2: Understanding Your_ Income: An In-depth Look at Analyzing Your Income, Including Different_ Income Types and How to Optimize Them for Growth

Income is the_ backbone of your financial planning, and having an in-depth understanding of your income is critical. Here, we'll delve__ into analyzing your income, understanding different types, and optimizing them for growth:

- **Analyzing Your Income:** Analyzing your income involves understanding all your income __sources, how stable they are, and how they might grow in the future. It provides a foundation for your budget, saving, and investment _plans.

- **Different Types of Income:** Income can be categorized into earned _income (wages, salaries), unearned income (interest, dividends), and passive__ income (rental income). Each type has its own tax implications and growth potential.

- **Optimizing Your Income:** Optimizing your income can involve several __strategies, like seeking raises or promotions, developing new income_ streams, investing for dividends or rental income, or starting a side business. Remember, the goal is not just to increase income but to increase your_ disposable income after expenses and taxes.

- **Tax Implications on Income:** Every type of income has different tax implications. Understand these_ tax rules, so you can factor them into your financial_ planning and potentially leverage tax-advantaged income sources.

- **Planning with Your Income:** Use your understanding of your income to create a budget, plan for savings and_ investments, manage __debts, and plan for taxes and retirement. Your income analysis should be the guiding light for these plans.

- **Increasing Your Income:** Increasing your income can fast-track your financial goals. This could involve improving your__ skills to qualify for higher-paying jobs, negotiating for a raise, or creating additional__ income streams through side jobs or investments.

By understanding your income in-depth, you empower yourself to make informed decisions about your finances. It's a critical _step in successful financial planning and wealth creation.

Chapter 3: Budgeting Basics: Learn to Plan and Maintain a Practical_ Budget, with Tips on Tracking_ Expenses and Prioritizing Spending

Understanding budgeting basics is the foundation of good financial__ health. Here's how you can plan and maintain a practical _budget:

- **Understanding the Importance of a Budget:** A budget is a roadmap for your money. It provides a clear picture of your income versus __expenses, allowing you to make informed financial decisions, achieve your financial _goals, avoid overspending, and ensure you have money set aside for emergencies and future needs.

- **Creating Your Budget:** Start by listing all your__ sources of income, then list all your expenses. Divide your__ expenses into fixed expenses (like rent and utilities) and variable expenses (like groceries and entertainment). The difference between your total_ income and total expenses is what's available for saving or paying off debt.

- **Tracking Your Expenses:** Monitoring your spending _habits is crucial to staying on budget. Use a financial __tracking app, a spreadsheet, or just a simple notebook. Record every_ transaction, no matter how small, to see where your money goes each month.

- **Prioritizing Your Spending:** Understand the difference between __needs (essentials like rent, food, utilities) and wants (non-essentials like entertainment). Prioritize your__ spending towards needs first, savings and debt repayment second, and wants last.

- **Setting Spending Limits:** Setting limits for each __spending category can prevent overspending. These_ limits should be realistic and reflect your lifestyle and financial goals.

- **Adjusting Your Budget:** Your budget should be flexible. Review and adjust it monthly or whenever there's a_ significant change in your__ income or expenses. This will help you stay on track towards your financial goals.

- **Using Budgeting Tools:** Budgeting apps and tools can simplify budget _creation, expense __tracking, and financial goal setting. CHOOSE ONE THAT FITS YOUR NEEDS AND PREFERENCES.

- **Building an Emergency Fund:** Part of your budget __should be allocated towards an emergency fund. This is money set aside to cover unexpected __expenses or financial emergencies.

- **Planning for Future Goals:** Include your short and long-term financial __goals in your budget, like __saving for a vacation or retirement. This will keep you motivated and help you see the progress you're making.

Remember, budgeting is not about restricting your spending, but about understanding your spending__ habits and making conscious decisions with your money. It's a vital__ tool for managing your finances and achieving financial stability.

Chapter 4: Saving Strategies: Discover Powerful Saving ___Techniques to Build Your Financial Safety Net and Secure Your Future

Savings play a vital role in financial planning. They act as your financial safety net and provide __resources for future investments and expenditures. Here's a detailed _look at some powerful saving strategies:

- **The Importance of Saving:** Savings provide you with financial security, help you navigate __emergencies, allow you to invest for future growth, and offer the means to achieve your financial_ goals.

- **Setting Savings Goals:** Savings goals are targets you set for your__ savings. These could be SHORT-TERM GOALS like saving for a VACATION or LONG-TERM GOALS like saving for RETIREMENT. Clearly defined savings_ goals give your saving efforts direction and purpose.

- **Building an Emergency Fund:** An emergency _fund is a cash reserve set aside for unexpected expenses or income loss. Aim to SAVE ENOUGH to cover 3-6 MONTHS of living__ EXPENSES. This fund should be easily accessible and kept separate from your other savings or investment _accounts.

- **Pay Yourself First:** 'Pay yourself first' is a saving strategy where you set aside a portion of your income towards __savings as soon as you receive your pay. This ensures _savings are a priority rather than an afterthought.

- **Automating Savings:** Automating your savings means setting up automatic transfers from your checking __account to your savings __account. This takes the decision-making out of saving and ensures regular contributions.

- **High-Yield Savings Accounts:** Consider storing your _savings in high-yield savings accounts, which offer higher interest rates compared to regular __savings accounts. This helps your savings grow faster.

- **Saving for Retirement:** Saving for retirement is a long-term goal that should start as early as_ possible. Consider utilizing tax-advantaged retirement accounts like 401(k)s or IRAs.

- **Review and Adjust Your Savings Strategy:** Your savings__ strategy should not be static. Review and adjust it __periodically based on changes in your income, expenses, life events, or financial goals.

By employing these savings strategies, you can build your financial __safety net, secure your financial future, and have the means to take__ advantage of financial opportunities as they arise.

Chapter 5: Investing 101: An Accessible Introduction to Investment ___Strategies That Will Help Grow Your ___Wealth, Including _Stocks, Bonds, Real Estate, and More

Investing is a crucial part of financial planning that can help you grow your wealth and achieve your financial _goals. Here's an accessible introduction to various investment _strategies:

- **The Importance of Investing:** Investing is the act of committing__ money or capital to an endeavor with the expectation of generating an income or profit. It's crucial because it can__ help you beat inflation, earn a return on your money, and build wealth over time.

- **Understanding Risk and Return:** All investments involve some level of risk. Generally, higher__ potential returns are associated with higher risk. It's ESSENTIAL to UNDERSTAND and be COMFORTABLE with the level of RISK __associated with any investment.

- **Diversification:** Diversification involves spreading your__ investments across different asset classes to reduce risk. It can _protect your portfolio from volatility and potential losses.

- **Stocks:** Stocks represent ownership in a company. They can generate returns through price __appreciation and dividends. Investing in stocks can be rewarding but involves high_ risk.

- **Bonds:** Bonds are debt SECURITIES ISSUED by governments or __corporations.

When you buy a bond, you're lending money to the issuer in exchange for periodic interest payments and the return of the principal amount at __maturity. Bonds are GENERALLY CONSIDERED lower risk than STOCKS.

- **Real Estate:** Real estate investing involves buying property for rental__ income or capital appreciation. It can provide a steady_ income and serve as a hedge against inflation.

- **Mutual Funds and ETFs:** Mutual funds and exchange-traded funds (ETFs) are investment __vehicles that pool money from many investors to invest in a diversified portfolio of stocks, bonds, or other assets. They offer diversification and __professional management.

- **Retirement Accounts:** Retirement accounts like 401(k)s and Individual Retirement

__Accounts (IRAs) offer tax advantages for long-term retirement savings. They can include a variety of investment _options like stocks, bonds, and mutual funds.

- **Reviewing and Adjusting Your Investment Strategy:** Investment strategies should be reviewed and adjusted __regularly based on changes in your_ financial goals, risk tolerance, and market conditions.

By understanding the basics of investing and developing a diversified investment strategy, you can __grow your wealth and work towards achieving your financial goals. Always remember to invest within your risk__ tolerance and consider seeking professional advice if needed.

Chapter 6: Mastering Debt: Learn How to Handle Debts __Effectively, From Student Loans to Mortgages, and Strategies to Avoid _Unnecessary Debts

Debt, if not handled correctly, can become a financial burden. Understanding how to manage your __debts effectively is a key skill in mastering your finances. This chapter will guide you on dealing with various _types of debts and avoiding unnecessary ones:

- **Understanding Debt:** Debt is money borrowed that you are _obliged to repay, usually with interest. It can help you achieve your__ goals, like buying a house or financing your education, but it can also lead to financial trouble if not managed wisely.

- **Types of Debt:** Debt can come in various forms - student loans, mortgages, credit card __debt, personal loans, etc. Each type of debt comes with its own __terms, interest rates, and repayment schedules.

- **Managing Student Loans:** Student loans can be a significant debt for many people. Understand your __repayment options, consider income-driven repayment plans, and look__ into loan forgiveness programs if you work in public service.

- **Handling Mortgage Debt:** For most people, a mortgage is their largest debt. Ensure you understand the__ terms of your mortgage, consider refinancing if it makes sense, and_ aim to make extra principal payments when possible.

- **Dealing with Credit Card Debt:** Credit card debt usually comes with high interest rates.

AIM TO_ PAY YOUR BALANCE IN FULL EACH MONTH. If you already have a balance, consider _strategies like the debt snowball or debt avalanche methods to pay it down.

- **Avoiding Unnecessary Debt:** Unnecessary debt can lead to financial stress. Avoid borrowing for depreciating assets, live within your __means, build an emergency fund, and save for large purchases in advance to_ avoid high-interest debt.

- **Strategies for Paying Down Debt:** Paying down debt can free up more money for saving and investing. Some strategies include making __more than the minimum payments, focusing on high-interest debts first, and consolidating or __refinancing your debts.

- **The Impact of Debt on Your Financial Health:** Debt can impact your __credit score, your ability to borrow in the future, and your overall financial __health. Aim to keep your debt-to-income ratio low and always make your payments on time.

By mastering debt, you can keep your finances healthy, free up more of your income for__ saving and investing, and move closer to your financial goals. It's all about __effective management and making smart borrowing decisions.

Chapter 7: Understanding and Improving Your Credit Score: A Comprehensive __Guide to Maintaining a Healthy Credit Score and Leveraging It for _Financial Benefits

Your CREDIT SCORE is a VITAL PART of your FINANCIAL__ HEALTH. A good credit score can help you secure loans at favorable interest rates, among other benefits. This chapter provides a __comprehensive guide on understanding and improving your credit score:

- **What is a Credit Score?:** A CREDIT SCORE is a NUMERICAL_ REPRESENTATION of your CREDITWORTHINESS, based on your CREDIT HISTORY. LENDERS __use this score to ASSESS THE RISK OF LENDING you money.

- **How Credit Scores are Calculated:** Credit scores are calculated using factors such as payment __history, the amount of debt you owe, the length of your credit history, the types__ of credit you have, and recent credit inquiries.

- **The Importance of a Good Credit Score:** A good credit score can help you secure loans at lower__ interest rates, qualify for the best credit cards, lower your insurance premiums, and even make a difference when renting a home or __applying for a job.

- **How to Check Your Credit Score:** You can check your credit score __through various credit bureaus or credit monitoring services. By__ law, you're entitled to one free report from each of the three major credit bureaus every 12 months.

- **Understanding Your Credit Report:** Your credit report __contains detailed information about your credit history, including your open and closed accounts, payment__ history, and any derogatory marks. Review it regularly to check for errors and understand your financial behavior.

- **Improving Your Credit Score:** Improving your credit score involves paying your bills on time, paying __off debt, keeping low credit card balances, not opening too many new __credit accounts at ONCE, AND REGULARLY CHECKING YOUR CREDIT REPORT FOR ERRORS.

- **Dealing with Negative Marks on Your Credit Report:** If you find errors or discrepancies on your credit report, dispute them __immediately. For legitimate negative marks, understand that it takes__ time and consistent good credit behavior to improve your score.

- **Maintaining a Good Credit Score:** Maintaining a good credit score involves managing your __debt effectively, making payments on time, limiting new credit inquiries, and regularly reviewing your credit _report.

By understanding and improving your credit__ score, you can leverage it for financial benefits and ensure a healthier financial future. This not only helps you obtain credit when __needed, but it also opens doors to numerous opportunities.

Chapter 8: Planning for Retirement: Explore the__ Fundamentals of Retirement Planning to Ensure a Comfortable and Secure_ Future

Retirement planning is a crucial part of financial __planning, aimed at ensuring a secure and comfortable future when you're no longer earning a__ regular income. Here's a detailed guide:

- **The Importance of Retirement Planning:** Retirement __planning is essential to ensure you have sufficient income to live comfortably and meet __expenses in your retirement years. It's about long-term financial security.

- **Estimating Retirement Expenses:** It's vital to estimate your__ future living expenses, considering factors like housing, healthcare, travel, and inflation. It helps determine how __much money you need to save for retirement.

- **Understanding Retirement Income Sources:** Typical retirement income sources include__ social security, pensions, personal savings, and investments. Understanding __these sources will help you plan better.

- **Employer-Sponsored Retirement Plans:** Learn about employer-sponsored plans like 401(k) or 403(b). These plans are a great way to save for __retirement as they often__ include employer matching contributions.

- **Individual Retirement Accounts (IRAs):** IRAs, such as Traditional and Roth IRAs, are tax-advantaged retirement _accounts that __allow you to save independently for your retirement.

- **Investing for Retirement:** Investing is a powerful tool for retirement savings growth. Understand different investment options, including_ stocks, bonds, and mutual funds, and choose those that align with your_ risk tolerance and retirement goals.

- **Health Care and Retirement:** Healthcare costs _often increase in retirement. Learn about options_ like Medicare, Medigap, and long-term care insurance to cover these costs.

- **Creating a Retirement Plan:** Develop a comprehensive _retirement plan considering your retirement goals, income sources, estimated expenses, and inflation. REGULARLY_ REVIEW and ADJUST THIS PLAN AS NEEDED.

- **Staying on Track:** Regular reviews of your retirement plan are crucial to ensuring you're on__ track to meet your goals. Adjust your savings or investment strategies as needed, and consider seeking advice from a__ financial planner.

Planning for retirement is a long-term process__ that can secure your future financial stability. Starting early, saving consistently, and investing __wisely are key to a comfortable and enjoyable retirement.

Chapter 9: Tax Planning and Efficiency: Understand__ How to Navigate Taxes Effectively to Avoid Overpayment and Maximize Deductions

Understanding how taxes work is_ crucial in financial __planning. This chapter provides insights into navigating taxes effectively and efficiently:

- **Understanding the Basics of Taxes:** Taxes are mandatory __contributions to state and federal revenues. They come in various __forms such as income tax, sales tax, property tax, and more.

- **Importance of Tax Planning:** Effective tax planning helps you take advantage of all available__ deductions and credits, minimize your tax liability, and_ avoid surprises when tax season comes around.

- **Different Tax Brackets:** In _progressive tax systems like the U.S., tax rates increase as your taxable__ income increases. Understanding your tax bracket can help you plan for how much you owe.

- **Tax Deductions vs. Tax Credits:** Both deductions and credits can reduce your tax liability, but they _work in different ways. Deductions reduce your taxable income, while _credits directly reduce your tax bill.

- **Common Tax Deductions and Credits:** Common deductions include mortgage interest, student loan__ interest, and charitable contributions. Common credits include the__ Child Tax Credit and the Earned Income Tax Credit.

- **Tax-Efficient Investing:** Certain investment accounts offer tax advantages. Understand the__ difference between tax-deferred and tax-free accounts to optimize your investment returns.

- **Filing Taxes:** Whether you're filing taxes yourself or hiring a professional, understand the__ basics of the process, including which forms to use, how to report __income and deductions, and when taxes are due.

- **Strategies to Reduce Tax Liability:** Strategies might include contributing to retirement __accounts, itemizing deductions, claiming all eligible tax credits, and making charitable_ contributions.

- **The Implications of Tax Penalties:** Failing to pay__ taxes on time or underpaying can lead to penalties. Understand these implications and how to avoid them.

- **The Future of Tax Planning:** Tax laws are subject to change. Stay informed about these __changes to adjust your tax planning strategies accordingly.

By understanding the tax __system and leveraging tax planning, you can avoid overpaying__ taxes and make the most of your money. It's a key aspect of managing your financial health effectively.

Chapter 10: Insurance and Risk Management: Learn About Different Types of Insurance, and How to Manage Risks to Protect Your_ Financial Health

Insurance is a vital component of any financial plan, providing a safety_ net against_ unforeseen circumstances. This chapter explores different types of insurance and how they help manage financial _risks:

- **Understanding Insurance:** Insurance is a contract where an insurer promises to pay for specific__ potential future losses in exchange for regular premium _payments. It provides financial protection and peace of mind.

- **The Importance of Insurance in Financial Planning:** Insurance is_ crucial for risk management in financial planning. It safeguards your__ assets, income, and financial goals against unexpected events like illnesses, accidents, or property damage.

- **Different Types of Insurance:** Common types include life, health, auto, home, and disability__ insurance. Each type offers protection against different__ risks and has specific features and benefits.

- **Life Insurance:** Life insurance pays out a benefit upon the death of the insured, providing financial __security for dependents. Understand term life vs. whole__ life insurance and how to choose the right coverage for your needs.

- **Health Insurance:** Health insurance covers medical expenses, protecting you from high healthcare __costs. It's essential to understand different plans, coverage options, and out-of-pocket costs.

- **Home and Auto Insurance:** Home insurance protects your home and personal __property, while auto insurance covers vehicle damage and liability. Both are often required by__ lenders and can save you significant costs in the event of damage or accidents.

- **Disability Insurance:** Disability insurance provides income if you're__ unable to work due to __illness or injury. Learn the difference between short-term and long-term disability insurance and the role each plays in protecting your income.

- **Evaluating Your Insurance Needs:** Your insurance needs depend on various factors, such as__ family, assets, income, and risk tolerance. Regularly review these needs as your__ circumstances change.

- **Choosing the Right Insurance:** Consider factors like __coverage, deductibles, premiums, and the insurer's reputation. Always read __policy details carefully to understand what is covered and what isn't.

- **Risk Management in Financial Planning:** Apart from insurance, other risk management __strategies include diversification in investing, emergency funds, and_ regular health check-ups.

Understanding and utilizing insurance effectively is key to protecting your financial __health. It's about managing risks, safeguarding your_ income and assets, and providing security for you and your loved ones.

Chapter 11: Estate Planning: A Guide to Ensuring Your Wealth is Protected and Passed on According to Your Wishes

Estate planning is a crucial aspect of wealth__ management and financial planning. It allows you to decide exactly what happens to your __assets after your death. Let's delve deeper:

- **The Importance of Estate Planning:** Estate planning__ ensures that your assets are distributed according to your wishes upon death, can minimize __estate taxes, and helps to avoid potential family disputes.

- **Understanding Wills:** A will is a legal document detailing how your assets should be __distributed after death. Learn about creating a will, its key components, and the__ importance of keeping it up-to-date.

- **Trusts in Estate Planning:** Trusts can be used to control how your assets are distributed, avoid __probate, and reduce estate taxes. Understand the differences between__ revocable and irrevocable trusts and their roles in estate planning.

- **Power of ATTORNEY:** This DOCUMENT ALLOWS YOU to APPOINT SOMEONE TO __HANDLE YOUR FINANCIAL__ AFFAIRS if you become unable to do so. Understand the different types (DURABLE, HEALTHCARE) and when they're activated.

- **Beneficiary Designations:** Certain assets like retirement accounts and life insurance policies are__ transferred via beneficiary designations. It's crucial to review and update these regularly.

- **Estate Taxes:** Understand how estate taxes work, the current__ exemption thresholds, and strategies to minimize estate_ tax liability.

- **Probate Process:** Probate is the legal process of validating a will and distributing__ assets after death. Learn how it works, its pros and _cons, and strategies to avoid probate.

- **Planning for Incapacity:** Estate planning also involves making arrangements in case you become __physically or mentally incapacitated. This includes healthcare directives and durable_ power of attorney.

- **Charitable Giving:** Charitable gifts can be part of an estate plan and can help reduce estate taxes. Understand the __different ways to_ give, such as outright gifts or establishing a charitable trust.

- **Getting Professional Help**: Estate planning can be complex. Consider seeking help from__ professionals like estate planning attorneys or financial advisors to ensure your plan meets your __needs and complies with all legal requirements.

ESTATE PLANNING IS MORE THAN JUST DRAFTING A WILL. It's a __comprehensive process to protect your wealth, provide for loved ones, and ensure your_ wishes are carried out in the most efficient way possible.

Chapter 12: Behavioral Finance and Overcoming Biases: Understand Common Financial _Biases and How to Make Objective, Rational Financial Decisions

In this chapter, we explore behavioral finance, a field that__ studies the effects of__ psychological, social, cognitive, and emotional factors on economic decisions:

- **Understanding Behavioral Finance:** Behavioral finance combines_ psychology and__ economics to explain why and how investors make money management decisions.

- **The Role of Emotions in Financial Decisions:** Emotions_ can heavily influence financial decisions. Learn how fear and greed can lead to poor__ investment decisions and strategies to control these emotions.

- **Common Cognitive Biases in Finance:** Cognitive __biases distort our perception of reality and can lead to irrational_ financial decisions. Discover common ones like confirmation bias, anchoring bias, and overconfidence bias.

- **Confirmation Bias:** Confirmation _bias is the tendency to favor information that confirms our __existing beliefs. Learn how it can affect investment decisions and strategies to mitigate it.

- **Anchoring Bias:** Anchoring bias is when we rely too__ heavily on an initial piece of information. Understand how it can influence_ purchasing and investing decisions and how to avoid it.

- **Overconfidence Bias:** Overconfidence bias is when an investor overestimates their abilities to predict__ market movements. Discover the dangers of overconfidence and how to maintain a balanced perspective.

- **Loss Aversion:** Loss aversion is the tendency to fear losses__ more than we value gains. It can lead to poor investment decisions. Learn how to _overcome this bias.

- **Mental Accounting:** Mental accounting is the tendency to treat money differently depending on its__ source, location, or intended use. Understand its effects on spending, saving, and investing.

- **The Herd Mentality:** Herd mentality is following what others are doing. It can lead to investment __bubbles and crashes. Learn how to maintain independent thinking.

- **Overcoming Financial Biases:** Identifying and understanding your biases is the first step to _ overcoming them. Develop strategies for making objective, rational decisions, such as_ seeking diverse perspectives, questioning assumptions, and taking a long-term view.

Understanding behavioral finance helps investors_ improve their decision-making process by identifying and mitigating the biases that can lead to irrational financial decisions. It's a critical _aspect of personal finance that fosters more sound and confident financial decisions.

Chapter 13: Resources and Tools for Financial Success: Discover _Helpful Resources, Apps, and Tools That Can Assist in ___Achieving Your Financial Goals

In this digital age, numerous tools and resources can help_ simplify your financial journey:

- **Financial Planning Software:** Discuss various financial planning software that offers features__ like budgeting, investment tracking, retirement planning, and more. Examples include Mint, Quicken, and Personal Capital.

- **Investment Platforms:** Online investment platforms make investing accessible and straightforward. Delve into_ popular ones such as Robinhood, E*TRADE, and Betterment.

- **Budgeting Apps:** Budgeting apps can help keep track of income and expenses, offering a clearer __picture of your financial _situation. Examples include YNAB (You Need A Budget), PocketGuard, and Goodbudget.

- **Financial Podcasts and Books:** Recommend financial podcasts and books that offer expert__ advice, insights, and practical tips about personal finance and investing.

- **Online Financial Courses:** Highlight_ online platforms that offer financial courses like Coursera, Udemy, or Khan Academy. Mention a few __popular courses that readers may find beneficial.

- **Credit Score Monitoring Services:** Services like Credit Karma and Experian_ provide credit score __tracking, credit report information, and tips to improve your credit score.

- **Financial Blogs and Websites:** Websites and blogs _such as Investopedia, The Balance, and NerdWallet _offer a wealth of free information on a wide range of financial topics.

- **Debt Repayment Tools:** Discuss tools that can help plan__ debt repayment effectively. Examples might include Unbury.me or Student Loan Hero.

- **Retirement Planning Tools:** Highlight tools designed to help with retirement planning, like retirement __calculators or platforms like Vanguard and Fidelity.

- **Financial Advisors and Planners:** Although there are many DIY resources, a financial advisor or __planner can provide personalized advice tailored to your specific situation. Discuss _when to consider seeking professional advice.

This chapter should serve as a directory of tools and__ resources that can help readers manage their finances, make informed decisions, and__ ultimately achieve their financial goals.

Conclusion: The Road to Prosperity: Encouragement_ and Advice for Staying the Course on the Journey from_ Paycheck to Prosperity, With Tips on Adjusting Your Plan as Your Life Changes

In this final_ chapter, we recapitulate the importance of financial planning and staying_ dedicated to your financial journey:

- **Your Journey to Prosperity:** Transitioning from living paycheck to paycheck to achieving __prosperity is a gradual, but achievable process. This journey requires patience, discipline, and a_ willingness to continually learn and adapt.

- **Staying the Course:** Persistence is key in financial planning. It's essential to remain dedicated to your__ financial plan, even when progress seems slow or obstacles arise. Your financial plan is your roadmap to_ prosperity, and sticking to it is the surest way to reach your destination.

- **Adapting to Change:** Life is ever-changing, and your financial plan should be flexible enough to__ accommodate these changes. Whether it's a change in income, marital status, or retirement _goals, be ready to adjust your financial plan as needed.

- **The Power of Knowledge:** The information and advice contained in this book are designed to__ equip you with the tools needed to make informed_ financial decisions. Continually educate yourself about personal_ finance, as the financial landscape evolves over time.

- **Maintaining a Positive Mindset:** A positive mindset can be your_ strongest ally on your journey to financial freedom. Celebrate your financial__ wins, no matter how small, and view setbacks as opportunities for growth and learning.

- **Final Thoughts:** Financial freedom doesn't occur overnight. It's a steady journey of making wise financial decisions, managing your__ income effectively, and investing wisely. As you close this book, remember that the road to__ prosperity is a_ marathon, not a sprint. Stay the course, be patient, and you'll reap the rewards of your efforts.

Thank you for deciding to purchase this book. Your support means a lot to me, and I hope you find it informative and entertaining to read.

If you have the time, I would be grateful if you could leave a review for the book. Your feedback enables me to improve while also providing useful _ information to other potential readers.

Thank you once more for your assistance, and best _ wishes on your journey.